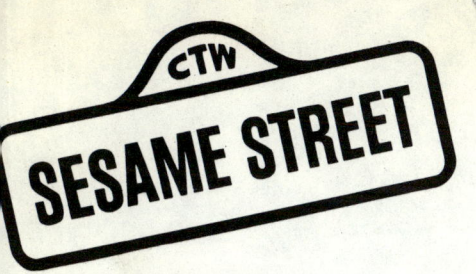

People in Your Neighborhood

By JEFFREY MOSS

Illustrated by LEON JASON STUDIOS

Featuring JIM HENSON'S MUPPETS

Based on the song, "PEOPLE IN YOUR NEIGHBORHOOD" © Festival Attractions, Inc. 1969, 1971, music and lyrics by Jeffrey Moss.

This educational product was designed in cooperation with the Children's Television Workshop, creators of Sesame Street. It has independent educational value, and children do not have to watch the television show to benefit from it.

Workshop revenues from this product will be used to help support CTW educational projects.

A SESAME STREET BOOK

Published by Western Publishing Company, Inc. in conjunction with Children's Television Workshop.

Copyright © Children's Television Workshop 1971
Muppets copyright © Muppets, Inc.
All rights reserved. Produced in U.S.A.
GOLDEN, A GOLDEN SHAPE BOOK, and GOLDEN PRESS® are trademarks of Western Publishing Company, Inc. Sesame Street and Sesame Street Lamp Post and Sign are trademarks and service marks of Children's Television Workshop.

Third Printing, 1974

WHO ARE THE PEOPLE IN YOUR NEIGHBORHOOD—
THE PEOPLE THAT YOU MEET EACH DAY?

Can you guess who always brings the mail
Through rain or snow or sleet or hail?

THE POSTMAN works the whole day through
To get your letters safe to you.

Do you know who sells the things you eat—
Like bread and eggs and cheese and meat?

No matter what you're looking for,
You'll find it at THE GROCER'S sto

Who's the man who works each day
To help to take the trash away?

THE GARBAGE MAN'S the man we mean,
And he makes sure our streets are clean.

Do you know who works the whole day long
To keep you feeling well and strong?

Who will drive you anywhere
When you get in and pay your fare?

Who's the one who always makes
Your bread and rolls and pies and cakes?

Who has scissors and a great big chair?
You sit in it. He cuts your hair.

THE BARBER snips and clips
and just won't rest
Until he's made you look your best.

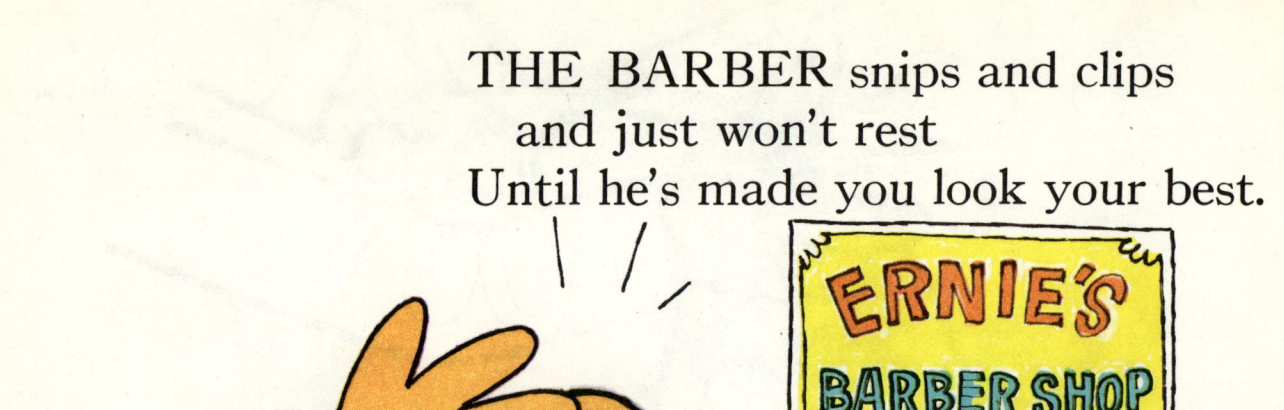

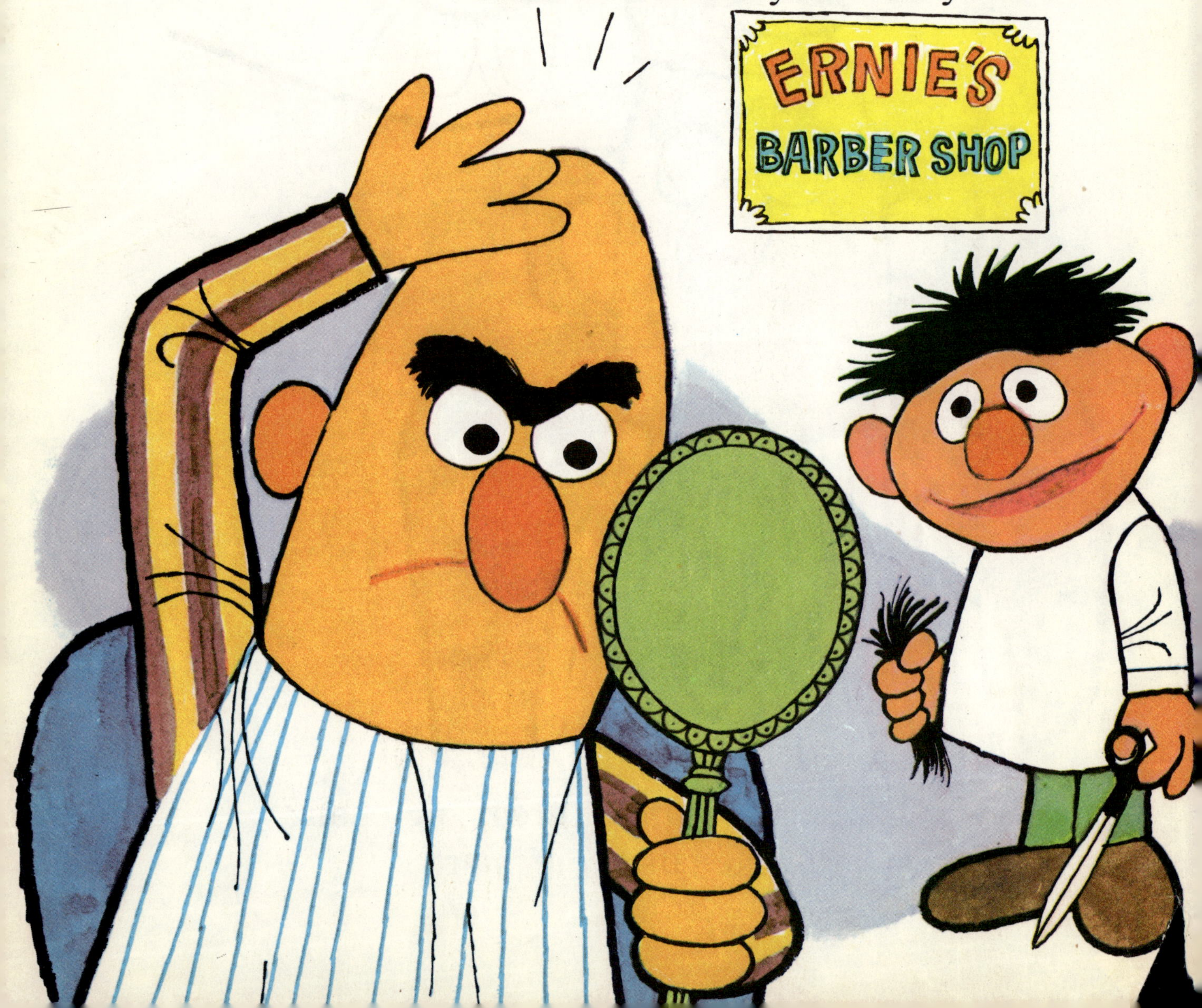

U.S. 1836349

Now, if you've got an aching tooth,
Who'll make it well—and that's the truth?

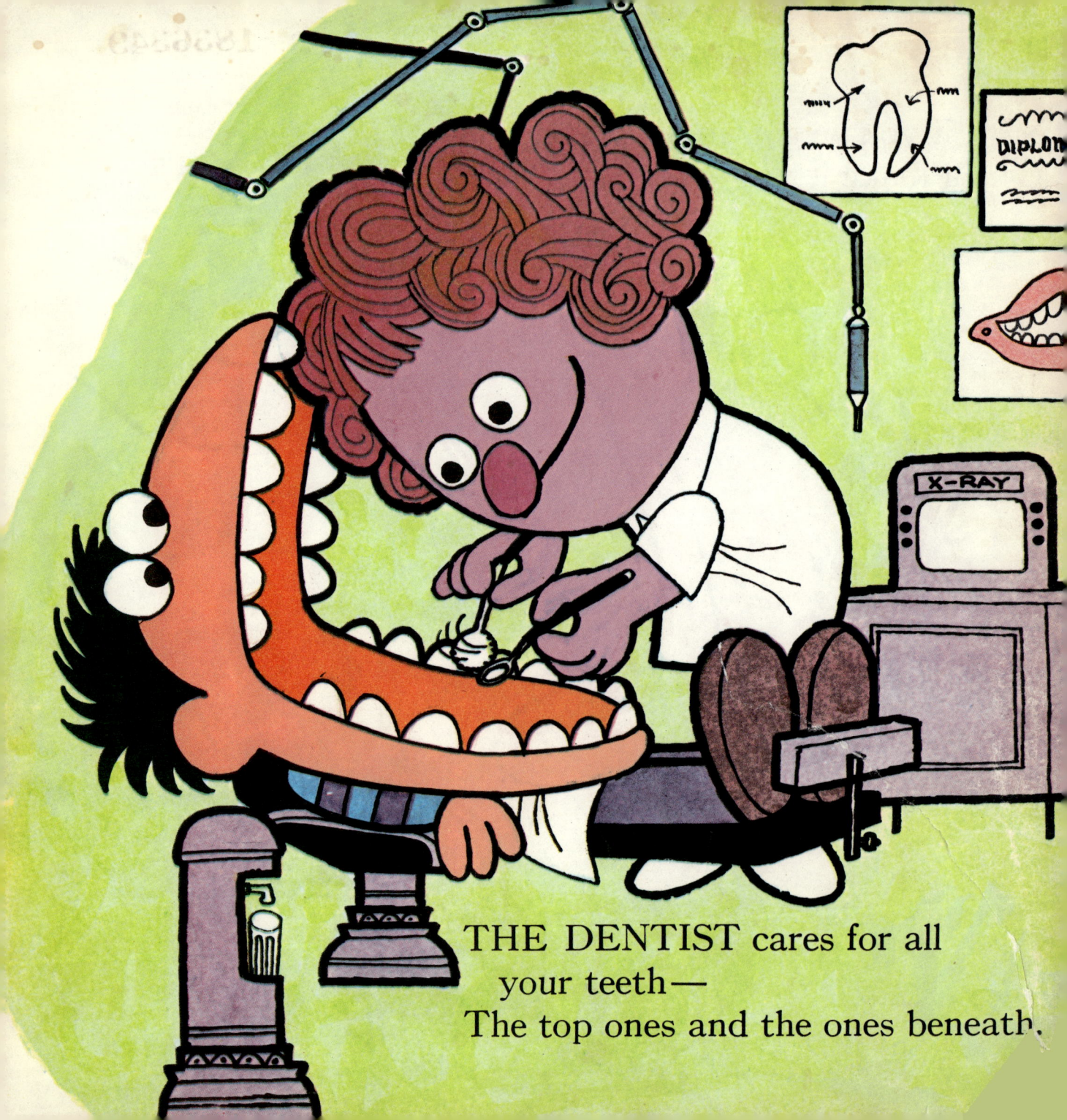

Whose engine is a shiny red?
He wears a helmet on his head.

If there's a fire anywhere about,
THE FIREMAN will put it out.